# No Visible Scar

Navigating your way through grief
in the wake of Covid-19 restrictions

Richard Littledale

Authentic

Copyright © 2021 Richard Littledale

27 26 25 24 23 22 21    7 6 5 4 3 2 1

First published 2021 by Authentic Media Limited,
PO Box 6326, Bletchley, Milton Keynes, MK1 9GG.
authenticmedia.co.uk

**British Library Cataloguing in Publication Data**
A catalogue record for this book is available from the
British Library.
ISBN: 978-1-78893-228-8


Printed and bound by Micropress Printers Ltd,
Suffolk, IP18 6SZ, UK.

# Contents

# Introduction

There is no version of my own life story which would ever have found me delivering a lecture in the Houses of Parliament. Not only that, but to deliver it on the subject of grief, and to do so from my own harrowing experience, was something which I had never wanted. Fifteenth months earlier on a drab November morning, my beloved wife, Fiona, had died at home. She was 53 years old at the time, and that summer had seen our thirtieth wedding anniversary come and go. To say we had 'celebrated' it would be an exaggeration. The cancer that was marching relentlessly through her body was a thief of many things – among them time, energy and joy. The anniversary was a necessarily muted affair.

Fiona was always more politically astute than me, and she would have loved to visit the Houses of Parliament. Now, here I was without her, looking out at the collection of peers, MPs and charity workers and telling them that 'bereavement is a deep wound with no visible scar'. I meant it. When you cope, people think you are fine, and when you don't, you try to hide it anyway. The result is that the scar remains invisible. To you, it is as obvious as the nose on your face. You see it every time you look in the mirror. You look through the window at an old familiar view, and you see it in the reflection looking back at you. It disfigures you on the inside, and affects your vision too.

Many have found that particular scar more hidden than ever in the time of a global pandemic. This season has seen us separated from each other in so many ways. It is as if we have found ourselves on an archipelago of thousands of tiny islands – all separated by the raging waters of Covid-19. We wave across the waters between us, but there is only so much you can communicate as you raise your voice across the distance. Are those arms waved in greeting or signalling distress, I wonder?

When the waters recede and those islands drift back together, will we recognize the occupant of each one, I wonder? Some have been changed forever by what they have been through. Many have experienced the traumatic excision of bereavement with no one there to hold their hand or hear their cry. Mourning has been done quietly and unobserved. Loved ones have been laid to rest with few to witness it. It is for those who have been through such things that this little booklet is written.

# 1

# Not Such a Good Bye

On television or in the cinema, people always seem to get the chance to say goodbye. As one slips away, so the other is there to hold their hand and say those precious things which need saying. Sometimes they are really important things about what has been or what will be. Other times, they may be the tender last words of love, perfectly articulated, from one to the other. Most times, the hero gets to say their last line – of defiance or reassurance or challenge. In truth, it is rarely that way and was not for me. While her long illness meant that Fiona and I had talked often about dying, her decline at the end was so fast that 'last conversations' were not possible. At some point during that longest night, I told her that it was OK to go and she nodded, but that was the last conscious conversation we ever had.

During the time of the pandemic, many have been denied the opportunity even to have that conversation. Often, a loved one has disappeared in a flash of blue lights and a haze of plastic visors and masks never to be seen again. Covid-19 restrictions have meant that bedside conversations, let alone a last embrace, have been out of the question. To be at home while a loved one is in hospital is always an acute source of anxiety. Usually, though, that anxiety can be assuaged by each permitted visiting time. We lurch from each hospital visit to the next, longing to see for ourselves how the person we love is doing. While staff have often made enormous efforts to facilitate video calls, they can never be a substitute for that face-to-face encounter. As the patient's condition worsens, so our own sense of desperation has deepened at our inability to offer comfort or even to see for ourselves how things are going. To hear that the person we love, now invisible to us, has died is the final confirmation of an uncomfortable truth: we were not there.

In other cases, the loss has been no more sudden than it would have been without the complications of the pandemic. We all know that people grow old and will eventually run out of years. However, the inability to accompany those in residential care through their last weeks or months has been a crushing blow. Loss is compounded by an insistent guilt which eats away at the mind and tugs at the heart. They were there for us when we were young, but we have been unable to be there for them when they are old. Knowing the sound medical reasons for these enforced separations has not made them any easier to bear. The sense that we have 'not said goodbye' somehow makes us feel less than human.

Of course, nobody really says goodbye these days. We may opt for its shortened cousin 'bye' or replace it altogether with 'see you'. Goodbye, though, has been relegated to the verbal archive – alongside 'gramophone' and 'telephone'. It's a shame, really. The phrase means 'God by ye' – and on the hardest days, having someone by you can make all the difference.

# 2

# Sent Off?

Funeral trends have changed a lot in recent years. The 'big send-off' is not what it used to be. Long cortèges of gleaming limousines bedecked with elaborate floral displays are a less common sight than they were. When I first started out as a minister, those big floral tributes and a funeral conductor walking in a tailcoat before the hearse was not unusual. Burials are now less common than cremations, and often an elaborate headstone has given way to a simple marker. Some of the changes are simply fashion, some are financial and others are a welcome sign that people have shaken off the obligation to 'do things as they have always been done'.

However, it is one thing to opt for change and another to have it imposed upon you. Before the coronavirus pandemic began, many of us might have welcomed the opportunity to work from home and spend more time in our gardens than we had done before. It all felt very different when we were *told* to do it, though. At that point, it was no longer our choice. People have been forced through circumstance into holding simple funerals, and for many it has felt like an imposition. During the time of the pandemic, funerals have been a very muted affair. Numbers have been restricted to ten or fifteen, spaced out in a room designed to hold four or five times that number. Families have had to make terrible choices about who gets to attend and who does not. Those who do not 'make the cut', or who have been forbidden to travel, have found that watching the funeral online makes them feel further away rather than closer. 'Peering into' the chapel to see a loved one's coffin on the same laptop where you send your emails and hold your video calls has felt both disrespectful and voyeuristic.

As a minister, what goes on in the chapel is my responsibility, but I know that it is by no means the most important part of the day. Hugging and embracing each other outside the chapel and letting the tears flow from eye to shoulder is vital. After that, the conversations which happen over refreshments and the happy memories which mingle with the sad are at least half a step to the world beyond the loss. These things have not happened. The enforced simplicity of these funerals has felt profoundly disrespectful. To say goodbye to someone special with what feels like no more than a whisper has felt like selling them short. In my years of professional experience, I have seen families tie themselves in knots about what Fred or John or Mary might have wanted – but most are sure that they would not have wanted this.

The promise of a 'proper' thanksgiving event at some point in the future does little to assuage the guilt or disappointment which they feel.

As I think of those in this position, I keep hearing the words of a grieving king in years gone by. In a prayer, he says to God that 'you have kept my tears in a bottle'.[1] If that still goes on, then there must be a lot of bottles now.

---

[1] King David in Psalm 56:8

# 3

# Drowned by Statistics

Do you remember the good old days before Covid-19 when we would roll our eyes at the latest Brexit headlines? There have been times during the pandemic when we would have given anything to listen to those headlines instead of the others which have filled the space. During this time we have become more accustomed to the statistics of death than at any point in our lifetimes. If someone had told me in 2019 that news bulletins in 2020 would include a daily death toll, I would not have believed them. The very idea that there would be regular briefings from 10 Downing Street on such things would have seemed unimaginable. 'Infection rates', 'R numbers' and 'mortality figures' have slipped unbidden into our vocabulary. We have learned to read the charts with their coloured lines denoting infections, hospitalizations and deaths.

The thing is, no number, either great or small, matters more to you than the one whom you have lost. A tally of three thousand, one hundred, or even twenty, means nothing when you only care about the one who matters most to you. Not only that, but the enormous numbers seem to make each single death recede into the statistical mist, as if lost among the numbers. The temptation to add the number 1 to the end of every Covid statistic is not inconsiderable.

On the one hand, you don't want your person to be just another number, and on the other hand you want their death to be counted and noted in every way. Numbers are somebody else's concern though. You don't deal in statistics, unless they are measurements of the seismic shock which has afflicted your particular world. At times it will feel as if you are the only one who remembers your person, carrying a candle for them which no one else can see. They may not have featured in the daily briefing, but to you their loss both encapsulates and eclipses all the others. For you, the scale of loss is measured not in numbers but in sorrows – no matter who else might be aware of it.

Do you remember how when lockdown started, we all commented on the birdsong? With fewer planes and less traffic, we could hear it all so much better than we ever had before. What happens to those singing birds when they die? Does anyone notice that the song is short by one voice, I wonder? Centuries ago, Jesus talked about 'not a sparrow falling to earth without God knowing about it'.[1] I suspect it would have to be a pigeon now, as they are so numerous. Either way, the point stands.

---

[1] See Matthew 1:29

# 4

## The Curse of Normality

I think there are two phrases which I would be happy never to utter again after this time in our lives. The first is 'you are on mute', which has become a stock phrase in every video call. The other is the phrase 'new normal' as if it were some state of calm and established peace. For a start, normal is neither old nor new. The word simply describes what is and therefore is neither old nor new. We will never reach a point where things become so static and settled that they never change again. Or at least, I hope we won't.

All the same, I understand the desire behind the phrase. As every week goes by, the pressure to get things back to the way they were increases. People want to laugh and hug and mix and shop and socialize in the way they used to do. They want to plan their holidays and hold their celebrations and look to the future with some hope in their hearts. All of that is completely understandable – and incredibly hard to embrace when you are grieving. When I was nearing the end of my bereavement leave after Fiona died, my anxiety levels about returning to anything which smacked of normality were through the roof. Some of that was simply because I was out of the habit. I had not been at work for four months, and I had not been at work without my best friend to support me for over thirty years. I was cautious and uncertain about navigating the landscape of work or of social encounters.

There was something more than that, though. The deep breath and resolve which it took to take that first step back into work meant that I was also taking a step away from her. Each new day as a widower put my days as a husband further behind me. Every little adjustment which I made to life without her felt like a small betrayal of my life with her. Some days, a small win in coping without her felt disloyal, although I know it wasn't. For you, that is all made much harder by the collective impetus to 'move on' and leave Covid, with all its bad memories, behind us. The future which you want to embrace has a gaping hole in it in the shape of the person you have lost.

Thankfully you are not alone. Anyone who has ever lost the person they love – whether to Covid-19 or something else, is familiar with that struggle. When comedian Oliver Hardy died, fellow funny-man Stan Laurel wrote in a letter to his widow – 'I miss him more than anyone will ever know, and I feel quite lost'. On the days when you feel that way, normal is over-rated.

Those are the days when I cling to an old verse in the Psalms which says that 'God is near to the broken-hearted'.[1]  I do hope so.

---

[1] See Psalm 34:18

# 5

## Slipped between the Cracks

I like my postman, and the dog likes him too. Far from barking at him, she greets him with a thrashing tail and would be more than happy to accompany him on his rounds. The postman is friendly, cheerful and generally brightens my day whenever he comes to the door. All the same, we did have one very awkward encounter. In the week immediately following Fiona's death, the amount of post rocketed up. Each day, he was pulling fistfuls of mail out of his sack to hand over to me. On one such occasion, he brightly quipped that it 'must be someone's birthday', and I had to explain that it was quite the opposite. It couldn't be helped, and we soon put it behind us. All the same, it was a powerful reminder that there are all sorts of signs to the wider world when somebody dies.

In a bygone era, of course, the principal sign would have been mourning attire. Dark clothes and veiled faces were a sign to everyone, both stranger and friend, that the person wearing the clothes was navigating the landscape of grief. The elaborate funerals of which we spoke earlier were another signal to the wider world that someone had died. Mourners, flowers and cars turning up at the house were all signals to even the most distant neighbours that a death had occurred. Repeating the news of your loved one's death is horribly draining. Every time you tell it again, it is as if you reinforce a reality which you scarcely believe yourself. These repetitions are hammer blows to the very heart of you – pounding, jarring and setting you on edge. Those outer signs saved you some of that costly effort.

Our isolated lives during the time of the pandemic have made many of these external symbols disappear. Mourners have been unable to show up at the house, and funerals have been such small affairs that they scarcely leave a ripple. Not only that, but when people have been working remotely at home, your absence from work for bereavement leave will have been largely invisible. People who return to work many months after losing their loved one will find themselves reliving it all again as they have to let people know that their life has changed. The alternative is to carry on as if nothing had happened, which carries the risk of things being more complicated further down the line.

The phrase 'heard it through the grapevine' originated with the early telegraph system when people thought all the supporting wires for the new-fangled poles made them look like the wires used for training vines. The phrase may be old, but the idea of allowing others to spread news for you when it helps is current. Perhaps some chosen friends and colleagues could help you to get this hardest of all messages along the grapevine, to save you repeating it?

# 6

# Eclipsed

It is the end of the evening news, all the grim statistics and political intrigues have been dealt with, and now there is just one story left. Somebody famous, usually from the arts, has died. Depending on the degree of their fame and the extent to which their death was expected, there will have been a video archive already prepared for just such a time as this. The video will roll with clips of their highs and lows. We shall see them in their prime and remember the sound of their voice or their glamorous looks. At the end of it all, the newsreader will repeat their name, in sombre tones, followed by 'who died today'.

I have nothing against commemorating those who have died. In fact, I have devoted considerable time over these past few years to encouraging people to do exactly that. All the same, these announcements can be terribly hard to watch. In my first couple of years after Fiona's death, I used to find these segments on the news so difficult that I would either shout at the television or turn it off. It was nothing to do with the person who had just been mentioned, and everything to do with the one whom I had lost. Every time I heard about their glamorous lives or their great achievements, I felt aggrieved because no one had ever mentioned hers. While they had been off making movies and writing songs, she had been changing the world in her own quiet ways – but the world at large knew nothing about it. The fanfare which accompanied their departure made hers seem all the quieter by comparison. It was as if they had eclipsed her.

This is a sentiment echoed many times during the pandemic, I suspect. Quite apart from the death of the one whom you loved getting lost in the statistics, it may also be overshadowed by more famous deaths. Each celebrity lost to Covid-19, while a tragedy to those who knew them, also serves to nudge your particular loss further out of the limelight. It is not intentional, not on anybody's part, but it does happen. To you, that special person will never be an 'also ran', but they can seem that way by comparison.

If you can bear to, then it may be worth devoting some time to thinking how you would feature them if they were on the news. What are the highlights you would pick out? How would you have shown them to the world? What would that last, lingering image have been on the screen as their dates were announced? Nobody will ever see this tribute, of course, but you are the only audience which matters in this case.

# 7

# Distraction Desert

Have you ever had a burglar or car alarm going off nearby, and there is not a single thing you can do about it? It nags away at you, shredding your nerves like the sound of a trapped bee. Grief can be like that – an insistent noise which it can be very hard to escape. It is there when you go to bed, there when you get up the next day, and quite often there all night in between too. 'My tears have been my food, day and night' is something that was written by a Psalmist long ago and still feels true today.[1] When I was first bereaved, I was astonished by how tired it made me. Some of that was tiredness accumulated from caring for Fiona in her last days. Much of it was the grief itself, though. Like that nagging noise of the alarm, it gave me no peace or respite. I would often find that I could not sit down for more than a minute or two without falling asleep.

That said, it was being awake which was the problem, and I was in acute need of distraction. Some days, I would go out to the shops two or three times just to be

---

[1] See Psalm 42:3

out of the empty house. Other times, I would deliberately split a project over several days, buying only some of the things I needed on each visit to the shops. The object of the exercise was to avoid spending too much time at home, which had become an uncomfortable place. Other people do the same, or maybe take holidays to visit places filled with memories, or visit new horizons to lift the spirits.

None of these things have been possible in the past year. Ordinary distractions such as shopping, and more elaborate ones such as holidays away, have all been out of the question. We have found ourselves marooned in a 'distraction desert', where the usual means of distraction are unavailable. The 'stay at home' message has been unequivocal but so hard to bear for those who would very much like not to be at home. For some, the very space which causes them the most anxiety has represented the borders of their world. This will not last forever, but for them it has lasted long enough.

When things got tough for Fiona and I, we often used to plan an escape route. Many times, it was deeply impractical and might involve anything from embracing a new career to living abroad. None of these things were seriously going to happen, but the planning of them in itself gave some relief from the here and now. You may find it is worth doing the same. What would you do, or where would you go right now, if you could?

# 8

# Behind the Mask

On the previous page, we discussed our need for distraction from the relentless, insistent voice of grief. Anything from a visit to the shops to a holiday abroad can help. Or at least, it could if it were permitted. Another thing which can help enormously is simply spending time with people. You don't have to do anything elaborate, and you may want not even to mention the name of your special person, but being with others can be a balm for the aching heart. Of course, even this has become more difficult than it was. Casual encounters, popping in to a friend or neighbour without appointment or agenda is a habit which we have lost. Once permitted, we may find it harder to pick up than we imagine. We are all creatures of habit, and a habit can be formed in a matter of weeks. Given that we have been living this pandemic life for more than a year, many of our habits have changed. The physical and social caution which has become second nature to us during this time will not be easily un-learned.

Up until the pandemic struck, most of us had rarely worn a mask of any kind. There might have been something occasional as part of a fancy-dress party. Some might have worn them for DIY, but they were not part of our lives. That is no longer the case. We have grown accustomed to the protection, and the privacy, which they provide. When I first started wearing mine, I would smile at people when I passed them in the supermarket – before realizing that they could not see my smile. A mask or face-covering reduces facial expression to the eyes and the eyebrows alone. The net result of all this is that we have all become more private people. We have grown accustomed to leaving our homes only rarely and to giving little away when we do. Exchanges with others in shops or businesses have necessarily been brief, and we have retreated from each other.

Your grief has been a far more private experience than it would ever have been before. In some ways, this may feel like a good thing. Sometimes, grief feels like such an indelible mark on your own soul that you feel as if everybody else can spot it a mile off. We talked earlier about it being an 'invisible scar' – but you may feel as if it is highly conspicuous to everyone, whether that is true or not. It follows you round like an 'aura', and some days you would just like to be you. Maybe the cautious distance which this time has imposed between us will allow you the space you need to come to terms with that scar. You will never lose it, but it will become part of you, like a big oak tree growing round a fence or lamppost.

For you, the physical and emotional caution which will mark our early encounters as we emerge from the pandemic may actually be helpful, giving you room to breathe.

# 9

# Untouched

One of the things which surprised me most during the early weeks of bereavement was that I experienced grief as a physical pain. It was a dull but persistent ache somewhere deep in my chest, and I simply could not shake it. I had thought that 'heartache' was a piece of fey nonsense created by singers and poets. It turned out that I was wrong. Sometimes the only way to escape from it was physical exercise – replacing the hurt with the ache of tired feet or stiff back, at least for a little while. Along with this physical sensation, there was another one. After about six months without Fiona, it struck me that I had not hugged anyone nor held their hand for months on end. It was as if touch, that most natural of human communications, had died along with her.

Of course, touch has largely disappeared from the physical vocabulary of our society. We no longer shake hands nor embrace each other. It has become second nature to give each other a wide berth on the pavement. We avoid things which other people have touched and recoil from crowded spaces in case we should touch accidentally. A physical reserve which had once been a national characteristic was on the wane, until now.

For many during the pandemic, the absence of touch began long before death itself. From the moment of diagnosis until last breath, many had to cope without the sight, let alone the touch, of their loved one. You may often find yourself troubled by the fading 'muscle memory' of how that person felt to you. You will find yourself dredging your memory in order to recall how their hand felt in yours or how their head felt on your shoulder. This is a normal part of grieving, but with a highly contagious virus the physical separation may have begun much further back. Your reach towards those physical memories is extended far beyond where mine ever had to be.

Centuries ago, King Solomon wrote in his 'Song of Songs' that 'many waters cannot quench love'.[1] I choose to believe that he was right. The enduring memory and impact of the person you loved does not depend solely upon your ability to remember them. The fact that you may forget from time to time how they felt or how they sounded does nothing to diminish the footprints they left in the world. Remember them as well as you can, but don't let physical amnesia fool you that they are truly forgotten.

---

[1] See Song of Songs 8:7

# 10

# Same Boat, Different Storms

It seems to me that the expression 'we're all in the same boat' is generally used by those whose boat is bigger, or sleeker or more seaworthy than mine. There is an implicit arrogance to the assumption that we know what someone else is going through or what they are feeling. There will come a time, in the not-too-distant future, when people will ask you whether the person you lost was a victim of Covid-19. When you say 'yes', some will nod as if they know just what that means. Statistically, those who died as a result of Covid-19 will all be seen as part of a larger whole. However, as we have said, no two deaths, nor the griefs which accompany them, can ever be the same. To you, the cause of death written on a certificate tells only the tiniest part of the story.

When the children and grandchildren of this time look back at what happened in the pandemic, they are sure to generalize. They will talk about numbers and trends and patterns, since that is how history is understood. There is nothing callous about it; it is simply a way of understanding a historical event from a distance. To see it as a mosaic of all the individual stories would be like trying to hold a video call with thousands of participants all speaking at once. It is simply too much to take in. This is why we deal in statistics when it comes to world wars or natural disasters – our minds simply cannot accommodate the detail.

For you, though, this whole story will always be understood through *your* story. For you, the human loss is measured in depth, rather than breadth. You do not believe your loss to be more significant or tragic than anybody else's, but you know that it is the one which matters most to you. Let other people talk in generalities. Let other people summarize the trends and statistics. For you, this pandemic will always have a face, and it is the face of someone you love.

When Paul Cummins and Tom Piper created their poppy installation, *Blood Swept Lands and Seas of Red* at the Tower of London, the impression created by the 888,246 poppies was mesmerizing. However, the greatest impact came from remembering that every single poppy represented a life. Long after the installation was dismantled, each poppy went to a new home. As they stand there now, in garden or on mantelpiece, they become an individual commemoration once again.

Your person, your poppy, is an individual human story, and will always remain so.

# 11

# On Digital Ghosts

I think we have all reached the point by now where we no longer specify that a meeting 'is online' as if that were a novelty. In fact, it is face to face meetings which are more unusual. We have all laughed and cried and discussed and shared online in ways which we had never done before. A time of lockdown and isolation would have been so much harder without the possibility of communicating in this way. Families and friends have been held together by this technology in ways never previously experienced. A hard time has been made at least a little easier by the digital revolution which has allowed us to stay in touch. However, there are disadvantages too.

People sometimes talk about a 'digital footprint', but what we have created is more like a network of tracks, criss-crossing the digital space, like animal tracks in the forest. Those tracks are made up of social media posts, videos, photos, screenshots and more besides. At the time, they are the very stuff of life – seeming ephemeral and generating a smile or a laugh. The thing is, they are not ephemeral, and many are still out there. They linger, like digital ghosts.

This means that you may well encounter the face, or voice or words of your loved one out there in cyber space just when you least expect it. I have WhatsApp groups on my phone which say 'Fiona left the group' which jar every time I see them. Somewhere in all the photos stored on there, I have a video of her coming down the stairs on a chair lift, which she had to use for the last couple of months of her life. I cannot bear to delete it, but then again, I cannot bear to watch it either. One day, I am sure, I shall be scrolling through the other things and stumble upon it when I least expect it. I shall brace myself.

Bracing yourself is the best approach here, I think. You cannot control the presence of this content, since much of it is not held in your hands. Better, then, to anticipate those days when you will come across it. Some days, it will make you catch your breath and shed many tears. Other days, though, the sight of that beloved familiar face or the sound of that voice may be just what you need.

There is a bench I have found in a nearby beauty spot which I have only discovered since losing Fiona. She would have loved it with its commanding view over the forest as it tumbles into the valley below. I have a problem with it, though. Inscribed across the back are these words: 'Those we love don't go away; they sit beside us every day.' As I sit there with half the bench unoccupied, I cannot agree. Some days, I am grateful for her lingering footprints in other ways.

# 12

# A Second Shielding

There are a lot of words which have crept into our vocabulary since this all began. 'Social-distancing' would be one, 'self-isolation' another, and 'shielding' too. Shielding, of course, has applied to the most vulnerable. The shielders have been the elderly, the fragile, those with underlying health conditions, or those who are living with anyone in those groups. In general, it sounds more positive than 'self-isolation' with its connotations of loneliness, but in practice it has been just as hard. To shield has been to keep yourself away from the world's possible intrusion into the safe space of your home. It has been to repel an invisible invader at the door that life might continue within.

Sometimes your grief will mean that you have to shield all over again. Out there, as people begin to mix once again, you will find that it can occasionally feel like harsh terrain. The sound of laughter, the clink of glasses and the music of casual conversation will all grate on you in such a way that you recoil from it. You are not being antisocial or cutting yourself off, you are just learning, very slowly, to live in company again. Like those emerging from their physical shielding, blinking in the daylight, you are emerging from your emotional shielding. Your steps are small, your heart is timid and you are understandably cautious.

Some days you will take a very deep breath and accept an invitation to coffee or a meal or an outing of some kind. To your own surprise, you will find that you enjoy it. It will feel good to be in company again, and you may catch sight of someone in the mirror whom you used to be. Other days, you will embark on such an outing full of anticipation, only to find that it is too much for you. Of course, you could make an excuse. Then again, it might be better just to say 'I'm not up to this today'. The people who invited you out did so because they care about you and are unlikely to be offended. We all need to learn to live with each other's fragility, and even more so after the things which we have all been through.

When the very first lockdown began, my local neighbourhood group produced laminated cards for everyone on the street to put in their window. The pink one said 'Self-isolating household: we need your help.' The yellow one said 'Self-isolating household: we are all fine for now, but please check again tomorrow.' You should feel free to use either of those messages with those who care about you.

# Postcards for You

Have you ever tried to catch a snowflake? They are fragile, delicate things – and likely to melt on your hand the moment you catch them. If they lingered, even for a moment, you would see that every single one is different. They are different shapes, different sizes, and utterly unique. The same applies to grief. No two griefs are the same. Even two people grieving for the same person will do it differently. In offering you my reflections, I would not want to suggest that my grief is the same as yours. I lost Fiona in very different circumstances to those in which you lost the person you love.

However, sometimes it can be helpful to have some company on a rocky road. That person will not tell you where to go, nor spend the whole time pointing things out so that you never get to see them for yourself. All the same, they are a little more sure-footed on this terrain, as they have been here before. Their insights may sometimes prove comforting – to pick up or put down whenever it suits you.

It is in this spirit that Authentic Media and I offer *Postcards from the Land of Grief* to you. In November 2017 I lost my wife and best friend to cancer, when Fiona died in my arms. In the days which followed, I tried my best to understand what had gone on but felt as though even the familiar places had turned strange. I was an unwilling visitor in a foreign land called grief, and felt all at sea. I started to do what we often do when we find ourselves in a strange place – I wrote postcards. These were not worthy treatises; they were observations on how it felt on that day to be in that place. They reflected the pain of the journey and the hope which continues to accompany me through it.

To my surprise, they seemed to strike a chord with many who had been there. A collection of them aired on BBC Radio 4's *Sunday Service* – and evoked a wide, global response. They then received an airing in the Houses of Parliament, as you know. In August 2019 they were published in a book, details of which are on the next page. The publisher's details are at the back.

I am so sorry that you are reading this booklet. I truly wish that you had never had cause to do so. However, I do hope that you can find some solace in this strange land called grief, even as I have done.

Richard Littledale

### Postcards from the Land of Grief

*Comfort for the journey through loss towards hope*

*Richard Littledale*

Losing a loved one can be a lonely, isolating and disorientating experience. Written as postcards from the land of grief, Richard Littledale honestly shares his personal experience in an accessible way that helps fellow travellers to identify their feelings and find hope in the foreign country of bereavement.

Thought-provoking, honest, gentle and ultimately hope-filled, this is a helpful companion for anyone dealing with loss.

978-1-78893-071-0

# About the Author

Richard Littledale is an author, preacher and pastor, and a regular contributor to BBC Radio 4's religious programmes.

After losing his beloved wife Fiona to cancer in 2017, Richard began to write 'postcards' to help him articulate his own experience with grief. The reaction to these on his blog and on BBC Radio 4's *Sunday Service* provoked such an overwhelming public response that they were later published as *Postcards from the Land of Grief*.

**Richard can be contacted via:**
Email: postcardprayers@hotmail.com
Twitter: @richardlittleda

# Authentic

We trust you enjoyed reading this book from Authentic. If you want to be informed of any new titles from this author and other releases you can sign up to the Authentic newsletter by scanning below:

Online:
authenticmedia.co.uk

Follow us: